Foreword by **Ross Burden**

Smell, touch, sight, hearing and taste.

We have all heard of the five senses, but did you know that food is something that appeals to all of the senses both individually and collectively?

Sounds strange, doesn't it? But, if you will give me a minute or two of your time, I will explain!

Ok, let's start with smell. Who hasn't become hungry walking past a baker's shop when the scent of delicious, warm bread is filling the air?

Need another example? What about touch? Some foods have such a fabulous texture that they make you want to reach out and touch them! Think of the smoothness of a peach or the rough, chunky skin of a pineapple.

Next up is sight. Whilst it might be the case that you can't always judge a book by its cover, most of us certainly judge a meal by its appearance. We have all seen beautifully prepared, artfully arranged meals in the photographs of glossy magazines. These dishes look so mouth-watering that we are often tempted to try them as soon as we get the chance in a restaurant or from the supermarket. It seems that these foods are saying to us "Eat me"!

Amazingly, food can even stimulate us through our ears. The sound of bacon sizzling in a pan or the noise made by a well known breakfast cereal when milk is added are just two that spring to mind.

Finally, after attracting our interest and exciting us by sending signals to one or more of our senses, the sensation finally arrives that our bodies have been anticipating... taste!

Food communicates directly with us as individuals, but we also use it to communicate with one another.

Whether it is preparing a simple meal for friends or family, or taking a loved one out to a posh restaurant for a slap-up meal, the message is clear, we are telling those people that we care about them.

Through food we can share our emotions and feelings and even our cultures.

What a fantastic way for the whole family to bond with each other by the shared experience of learning to sign and cook together.

So you see, there are more ways than just speech to talk to one other.

As someone who is very often paid to talk for a living, I found it utterly fascinating to discover just how easy it was to learn a new way to communicate by using my hands and facial expressions.

This book has helped me to appreciate that learning sign language is not only simple, but fun too.

What a fantastic way for the whole family to bond with each other by the shared experience of learning to sign and cook together.

Happy Cooking!

Ross Burden

Ross, celebrity chef and star of BBC's Ready Steady Cook

Introduction by Garry Slack

Welcome to Learn to sign and cook with Olli.

By combining the themes of food and sign language, this book will help children of all ages to improve their communication skills whilst they learn about food and how to prepare it safely.

Olli will help you to learn the signs associated with food and its preparation and then put those skills into practise by showing you how to prepare the mouth-wateringly fun dishes that Olli and his family have chosen from the monkey family cook book.

Olli says:
Let's learn about food and sign language together and cook up some fantastic recipes from my family cook book.

ISBN 978-0-9554932-1-8

Olli's Menu

Why learn to sign and cook?

Cooking is not just about preparing tasty meals. As any chef will tell you, the art of bringing a dish to the table requires lots of different skills.

For example, first the chef will need to plan the menu, often by studying recipes, whether they are from a book or researched via another method such as the internet.

It is essential to make sure that the ingredients complement each other whilst providing a balanced diet.

Next, our prospective chef might need to compile a shopping list, work out a budget and then go out and shop for any items not already in the kitchen cupboard.

Back in the kitchen, the ingredients will need to be prepared, weighed and measured to make sure that there are sufficient quantities and that everyone has an equal portion. Once the ingredients are ready, cooking can begin. This brings another factor into play - successful cooking is often about timing, by making sure that each part of the meal is ready at just the right time.

So, not only does a chef make use of his or her planning and literacy skills to decide upon the menu and read the recipe, but his or her numeracy skills are used for the shopping, portion calculations and timing of each stage of the cooking process.

In all of this hectic activity let us not forget what possibly is the most important skill of all... communication!

In commercial kitchens, such as those found in hotels and restaurants, communication between the chef and the kitchen team is vital to ensure that each dish is properly cooked and served on time to hungry, paying customers.

What better, more natural way to communicate in this hot and noisy environment than by using sign language?

Good literacy and numeracy skills and the ability to communicate clearly and effectively are so important to children and young people to enable them to succeed in later life.

This book will help children to develop these key skills and increase their knowledge and understanding of not only sign language, but also of food, its safe preparation and cooking.

Cooking is an activity that both child and carer can share together. It is this mutual experience, where both participants increase their skills and learn together, that can help to create a closer bond and understanding between child and carer.

Many of the signs associated with food are very easy to learn. Often a person who has no previous experience of sign language is able to quickly grasp why a particular sign represents a type of food.

The signs in this book are so simple and fun to learn that whether you already know some sign language or are a complete beginner, with Olli's help, you will soon be signing with confidence while producing fantastic meals for your friends and family!

Benefits of learning to sign and cook

Increases communication skills

By introducing new signs based around the themes of food and cooking, this book helps to build on a child's existing knowledge of sign language. This will help to expand their vocabulary of signs and increase their communication skills.

Strengthens the bond between child and carer

Participating together in an activity such as learning to sign or preparing a meal helps to bring child and carer closer together. Shared activities and experiences are an important foundation for a good relationship.

Teaches a child basic skills

Learning to cook teaches children many skills that are essential for life. These basic skills include numeracy, literacy and language. For example, a child will require a good grasp of numeracy to calculate how much of an ingredient is needed for a particular dish. Literacy comes into play when a recipe needs to be read and followed in a particular order, and of course language skills are needed to ensure that there is clear communication with others.

Improves coordination

Both sign language and cooking require manual dexterity. Sign language requires accurate hand movements to produce the signs, whilst safe knife handling skills are vital when preparing food.

Stimulates an interest in food

Today many of us lead such busy lives that frequently we rely on pre-prepared or pre-cooked food for convenience. Teaching a child to cook helps to arouse their interest in food. Children love to cook and will readily eat a meal that they have prepared themselves. This direct contact with food, from recipe to plate, can help to combat 'fussy eating'.

Helps raise awareness of hygiene and safety

In order to ensure safety in the kitchen, every cook has to know and follow a few simple, but essential rules. These include health and safety issues, ranging from basic hygiene such as washing your hands and keeping your working area clean, to more advanced matters such as making sure that food is stored at the correct temperature. As a child progresses and becomes more skilful in the kitchen they will increase their awareness of the importance of safety in the kitchen environment.

Cooking and communication are essential life skills

Learning to cook means a child can make a choice about the food that he or she eats and removes the reliance on convenience foods, encouraging a healthy diet. Good communication skills allow a child to interact effectively with the world around them.

Olli says:
Now I can cook,
I can choose the foods that
I want to cook and eat.
Recipes
Cooking
+
sign language
= FUN!

Hints and tips

Experiment
A cooking session is a good opportunity to try out new foods with your child and test your signing abilities. Learn the signs from a particular food group and experiment using those foods in new recipes. Then test your memory of signs. For example, how many things can you sign that would make a good topping for a pizza?

Plan a menu together
Practise finger spelling the items on your list to each other without using your voices. This will help with not only your literacy skills, but also your productive and receptive finger spelling.

Go shopping!
Going to the shops or market is a fantastic opportunity for you to practise the different signs for the foods that you see and also a great way to increase your child's numeracy skills.

Try signing the cost of each item that you buy, using the "let's finger count" section of this book to help you.

A silent meal!
Mealtimes can be chaotic and noisy affairs, often conducted against the distracting background of the ever present television.

Tell the family that for twenty minutes no talking is allowed. Family members must communicate with each other only by using sign language.

Each person must describe their meal and try to communicate how it tastes.

For example, they should sign what is on their plate and whether it is hot or cold, sweet or bitter, etc.

This enforced silence will really help to improve your concentration levels and sign language skills. Remember to get the other persons attention first by waving or tapping them gently and to maintain eye contact.

Become a collector
Collect recipes from magazines, television, the internet or even friends and family. Make a card index file or scrapbook of your favourites. Remember to file them in A to Z order – you could even use the finger spelling alphabet to help you categorise the recipes!
Soon you too will have a family recipe book just like the monkey family!

Get everyone involved
Make cooking a family affair!
Toddlers can be involved in preparing a meal by washing the fruit and vegetables, stirring cake mixture or even helping with the washing up!

Older children can improve their receptive sign language skills, literacy and numeracy if you turn off your voice and sign key parts of the recipe to them such as the ingredients, amounts to be weighed and cooking times, etc.

Game on!

Test your memory skills by playing this 'shopping list game' with your friends. This game can be played by just two players, but the more people who play, the more fun and confusing it gets!

The first player begins the game by saying "I went shopping and I bought" then signs an item of food. Then next player repeats the sentence and adds an item of their own to the shopping list.

For example, the first player says,
"I went shopping and I bought six eggs" (signs 'eggs' - although, if you want to make it really hard you can sign the number of items that you bought too).

The second player then says,
"I went shopping and I bought six eggs and a pizza" (signs 'eggs' and 'pizza').

The third player then says,
"I went shopping and I bought six eggs, a pizza and an onion" (signs 'eggs' and 'pizza' and an 'onion'). Each player should sign the words 'I' (point at yourself) and 'shopping' together with each of the food items on the list.

Players take it in turns to add items to the increasingly lengthy list whilst trying to remember the items and signs that went before.

This can be really difficult when you have twenty or more items to remember!

Olli says:
Why not test your memory skills by playing this brilliant 'shopping list game' with your friends.

How to use this **book**

This book can be divided into two sections. The first part deals with kitchen safety and healthy eating and focuses on the signs relating to food and its preparation.

The signs for food and food related words have been split into different categories according to either the food groups to which they belong or whether they are an equipment or preparation sign.

How to learn the signs

At the back of the book is an alphabetical index of all the signs. You may wish to learn the signs in that order or perhaps you may prefer to learn them in sections, concentrating on learning a few signs at a time from each group.

This is a good way to slowly build up your vocabulary of signs by learning in manageable 'chunks'.

If you are learning with a friend, why not each study the signs from a particular food group and then test each other to see how many you can remember.

All of the photographs and descriptions in this book are shown and described from a right handed person's perspective. If you are left handed simply reverse the instructions.

To produce any of the signs, begin by looking at the picture and replicate the positions and shapes of the hands, arms, body and facial expressions. Then read the description which explains how to perform the sign. Arrows on some of the pictures help you to see how the hands should move and in which direction.

The monkey family cookbook

The second part of the book features recipes that have been specially chosen by Olli from the 'monkey family cookbook'. Each recipe has been specially selected because it is fun and easy to make.

Of course, Olli will be on hand to encourage you in the kitchen and offer some fascinating food related facts!

Fantastic! Want to go a little higher?
Ok, here goes...

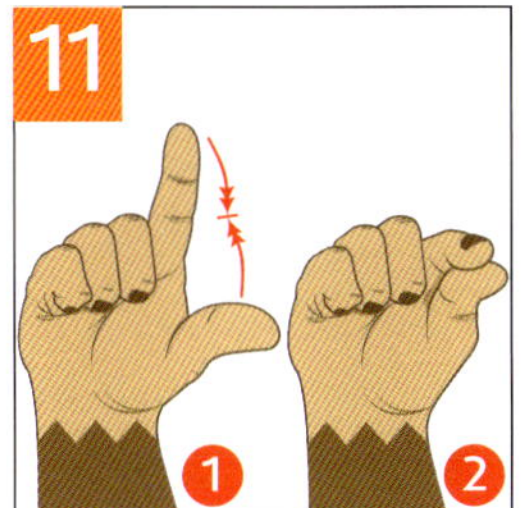

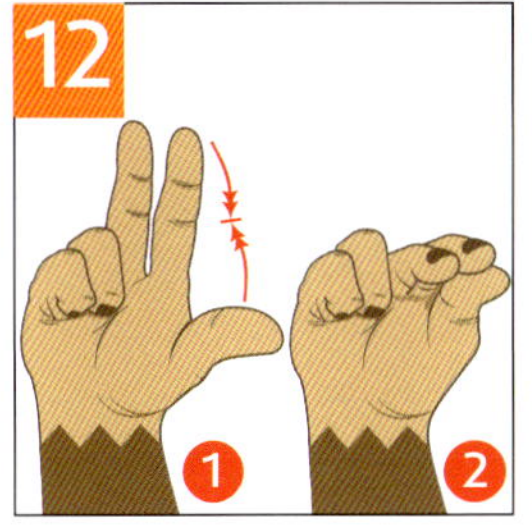

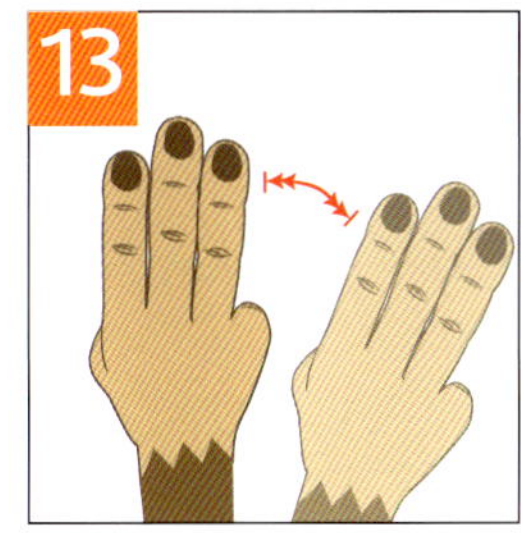

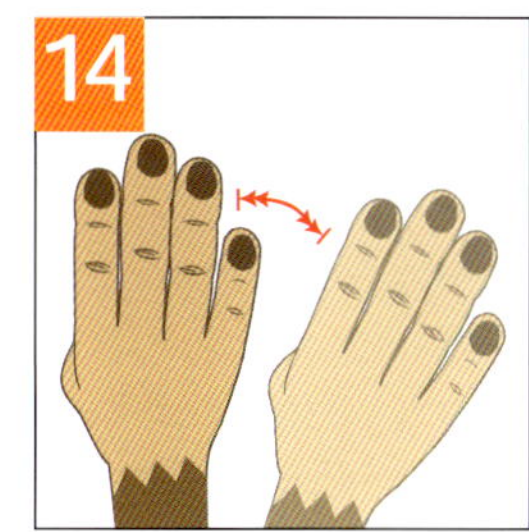

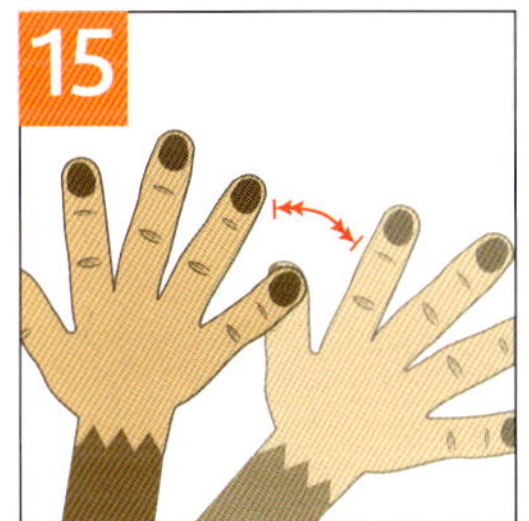

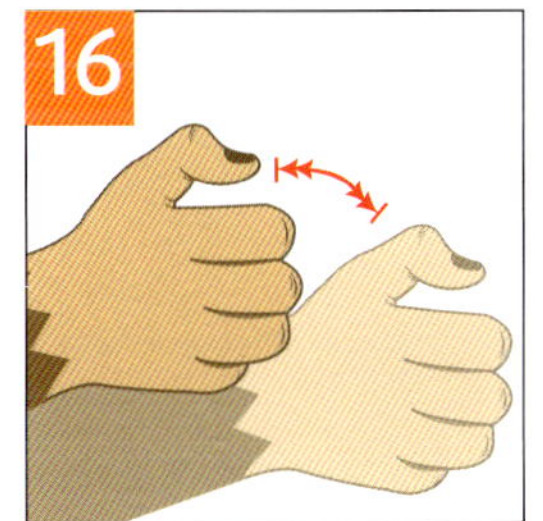

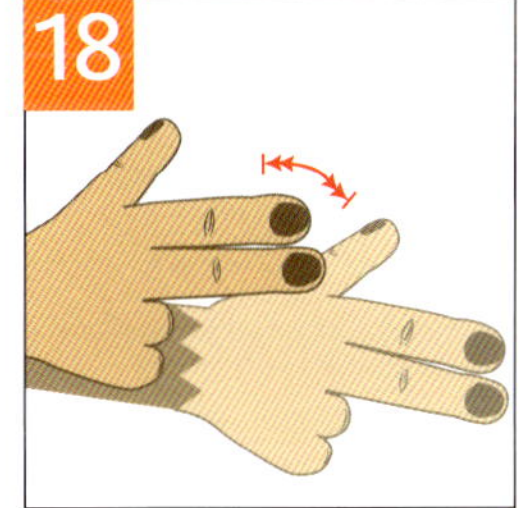

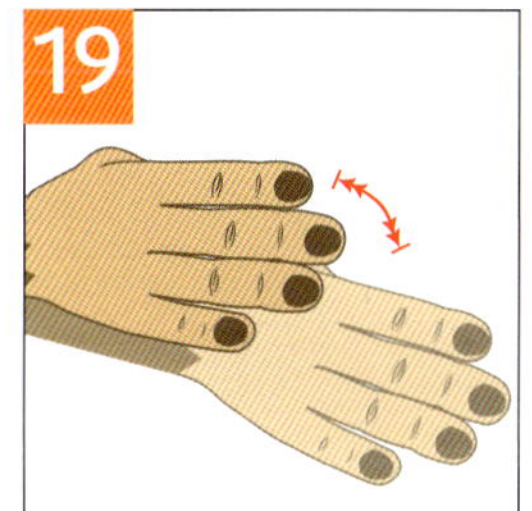

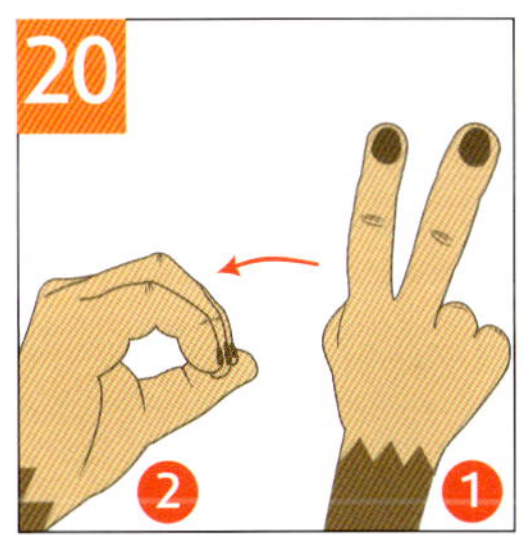

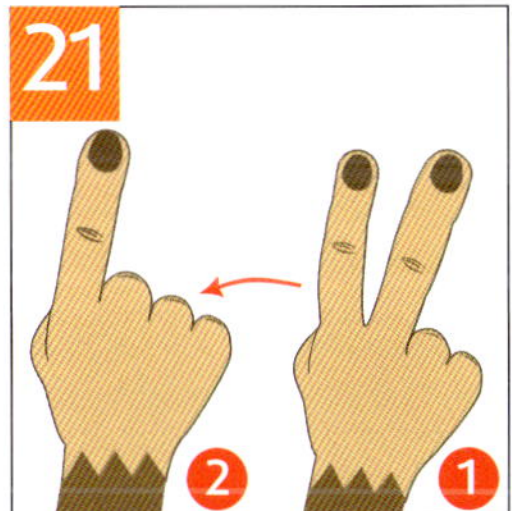

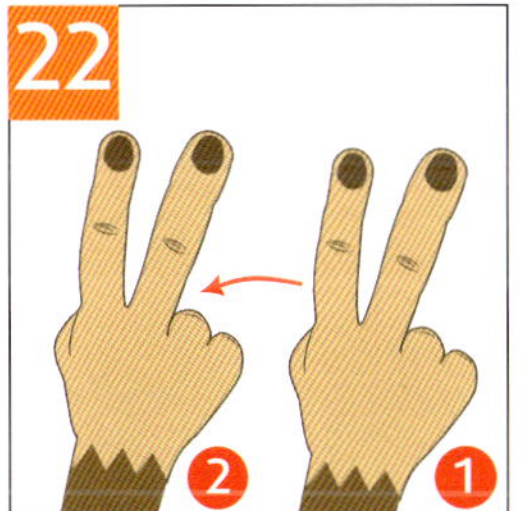

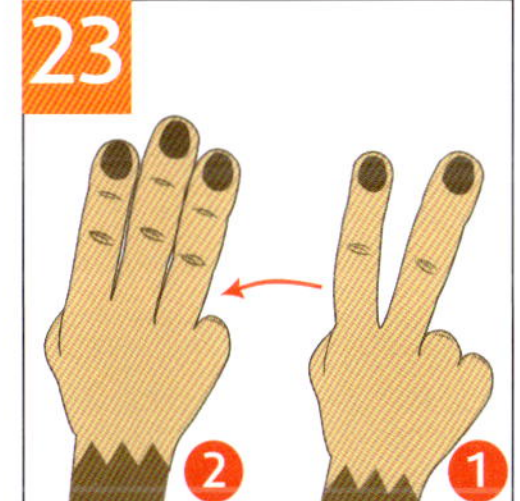

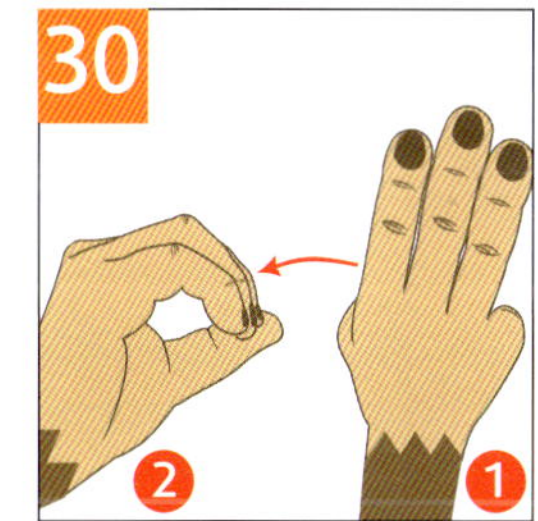

What about those really big numbers?

Make sure the right hand taps the left shoulder with the thumb twice for the second part of 1000.

Finger Spelling

Finger spelling is the backbone of sign language. It can be used to spell the names of people, places and objects. In British Sign Language, both hands are used to create the 26 letters of the alphabet.

M
N
O
P
Q
R
S
T
U
V
W
X
Y
Z

Welcome to **Olli's** kitchen

Cooking is so much fun, but my kitchen has a few basic rules that you must follow to help keep you safe and healthy.

Before you can start cooking any of the recipes from the 'monkey family cookbook' you are going to need a few pieces of equipment that can usually be found in most kitchens.

Watch out!

Whilst there might not be any crocodiles in my kitchen, it can still be a dangerous place. The kitchen is full of things that can hurt or injure you, such as heat, boiling liquids and sharp knives. Make sure that you have an adult with you when you are in the kitchen.

When looking at the recipes watch out for this symbol. It means you need to be extra careful and that you should ask an adult for help.

CAUTION

Olli's kitchen rules...

- Make sure that an adult is with you.
- Read the recipe through first to make sure that you really understand it and that you have all the ingredients and equipment that you will need.
- Never leave the kitchen when the grill, or hob rings are switched on in case they overheat or catch fire.
- Electricity can be dangerous, so don't touch electrical equipment or plugs with wet hands to prevent electric shocks.
- Don't play with your pets while you are cooking. Animals shouldn't be in the kitchen because they can carry dirt or pests and you might trip over them.
- If you have cuts or sores on your hands cover them up with a plaster to stop germs getting into the food.
- Don't cough or sneeze over food and wash your hands regularly, especially after touching your hair, mouth or nose and in between touching raw and cooked foods.
- To help stop the spread of germs and bacteria use separate chopping boards and knives etc for preparing raw and cooked food, or wash up the chopping board each time you use it.
- Be careful with sharp knives and edges. Never walk around carrying a knife and when washing up watch out for any knives in the bottom of the washing up bowl or sink in case you cut yourself accidentally.
- When tasting food, don't just dip in a finger! Use a clean spoon instead.
- Clear up as you go along – it's much easier that way!
- To avoid germs always use clean equipment and wash up afterwards.

Olli says you will need these things in your kitchen

- Large and medium mixing bowls (the large one should be heat proof)
- Small bowl
- Sieve
- Small vegetable knife
- Table knife
- Teaspoon
- Baking tray
- Wire cooling rack
- Chopping board
- Palette knife or spatula
- Wooden spoon
- Cheese grater
- Medium sized saucepan
- Food processor or blender
- Lolly moulds
- Paper cake cases
- Scales
- Liquidiser
- Measuring jug
- Oven gloves

- Don't leave food uncovered on the worktop as it can attract pests such as flies who could lay their eggs on it. Left over hot food should be cooled as quickly as possible and then covered and put into the fridge to prevent germs and bacteria breeding.

- Always wash your hands and put on an apron before handling food or cooking.
- It's easy to accidentally knock over a pan of something boiling or hot, so make sure that saucepan handles are turned inwards so that they don't stick out.

- Always use oven gloves when handling hot items and be sure to put them onto a heat proof mat or rack. Watch out for hot steam as this can burn you too.
- Remember to turn off hob rings, the grill or the oven when you have finished so that nobody can accidentally burn themselves.

- Mop up any spills on the floor straight away so that you don't slip on them.
- Make sure food is thoroughly cooked before serving it, because food that isn't cooked properly can make you very ill.

Olli says:

It's important to remember to wash your hands and gather everything together that you will need for a recipe before you start cooking.

Messy Iggi

My big brother Iggi can be so lazy and messy! Sometimes he can't be bothered to do things properly.

When he comes home late he likes to make himself a snack, but he can be a bit scatter- brained and often forgets to follow the rules of my kitchen!

Help Iggi learn how to be safe and healthy by seeing how many dangers and hazards you can spot lurking in the kitchen.

Recipes
IGGI is Messy!

Kitchen hazard **answers**

How many kitchen hazards did you spot? Check your answers...

1. Iggi has dirty hands and is not wearing an apron. It is important to be clean because germs can spread easily.
2. There is hot steam coming from the kettle. This could burn you. Also, be careful not to touch the plug with wet hands to prevent elecric shocks.
3. There is rubbish left round the bin. Someone could trip on it or it could attract germs or pests.
4. There is a banana skin on the floor – someone could slip on it.
5. There are liquid spills all over the floor. It would be easy to slip over.
6. The pan is boiling over and has caught fire. You should never leave a pan unattended as it could easily catch fire.
7. The handle of the pan is facing into the room where someone could easily knock against it, spilling the boiling liquid over themselves.
8. One of the hob rings has been left on, it could catch fire or you could burn yourself.
9. Diggi, the family dog is in the kitchen. Pets should not be allowed into the kitchen because they could spread germs or you could trip over them.
10. Meat has been left out on the worktop. It might attract germs and flies.
11. Spills on the worktop have not been wiped up. This could encourage the spread of germs.
12. The loaf of bread has been left uncovered. The crumbs could attract mice or rats.
13. There is a sharp knife left out on the work surface. Knives are dangerous.

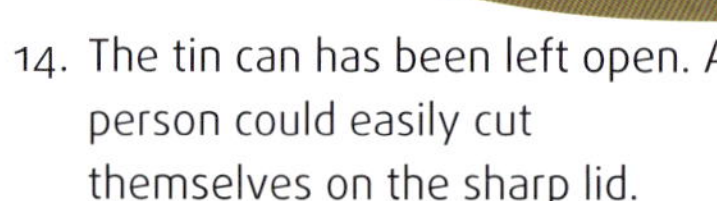

14. The tin can has been left open. A person could easily cut themselves on the sharp lid.
15. Iggi has not done the washing up. You should clear up as you go along.

Vroom, **vroom!**

Your body is just like the engine of a high performance sports car. But to make sure that it keeps working properly, and can win the race, it needs different types of food.

Staying fit and well means eating a healthy, balanced diet and getting plenty of exercise.

The food that we eat can be divided into five different groups;

- Fruit and vegetables
- Meat, poultry, fish, nuts and eggs
- Bread, rice, cereals pasta, pulses and potatoes
- Milk and dairy foods
- Fats, oils and sugars

Each group helps to give our bodies the things that it needs to stay healthy. All the food groups provide us with something different.

Just like a Formula 1 racing car runs on top quality fuel, your body needs the best possible nourishment to help it develop and stay in tip top shape.

To make sure that you get the right balance of foods from each group in your diet, take a look at the fuel gauge on the dashboard of my sports car on the next page. It has been divided up into slices to show you how much of the things that you eat should come from each of the groups.

Vroom, **vroom!**

If you want to race past the winning post, you need to make sure that you give your body the finest fuel! Try and be certain to take in foods from each group everyday. That means eating plenty of fruit, vegetables and energy foods like bread and pasta and fewer sweets and fatty foods. Sometimes this can be tricky!

Like lots of monkeys I have a very sweet tooth! I love things like cakes, biscuits and lemonade and even though I don't need them to stay healthy, a few of these treats now and again help to stop food from being boring.

But, as much as I like sweet things, I know that it's really important to eat lots and lots of fruit and vegetables, because they are so good for me. I always try to eat five portions of fruit and vegetables everyday, do you?

Olli says:
Five good portions everyday
Helps to keep the doctor away
To stay healthy and alive
You must eat well and exercise!

Munch a rainbow

Have you ever noticed how colourful fruit and vegetables are? They come in almost every colour of the rainbow and are packed full of vitamins, minerals and fibre!

Next time you go shopping, see how many colours you can spot and sign for the different fruits and vegetables that you see. Here are just a few. Can you think of any others?

Green: broccoli, kiwi fruit, limes, green apples, grapes, pears, cabbage, green beans, peas, green peppers, cucumbers, spinach and celery.

Red: cherries, strawberries, raspberries, red peppers, beetroot, tomatoes, red apples and radishes.

Yellow and Orange: grapefruit, melon, oranges, pineapples, carrots, yellow peppers, lemons and bananas.

Purple and Blue: blueberries, plums and purple grapes.

Why not try and eat a piece of fruit or vegetable from each of the colours everyday? You could even make yourself a wall chart to hang in the kitchen to keep track of your progress. Every time you feel peckish look at your chart to see what colour fruit or vegetable you need to eat to complete your target for the day.

Food preparation signs - vocabulary

Barbecue
Two hands, palms facing, with index and middle fingers extended in a 'V' shape twist at the wrists twice as if rotating meat on a spit.

Bottle
Right hand fist with thumb extended makes contact with the lips and head tilts back as if drinking from a bottle.

Boil
Hands with index fingers extended and pointing upwards move up and down alternately in small circles to mimic boiling water.

Bowl
Cupped hands mime the shape of a bowl.

Chef
Two 'N' hands on either side of the head move upwards to outline the shape of a chef's hat.

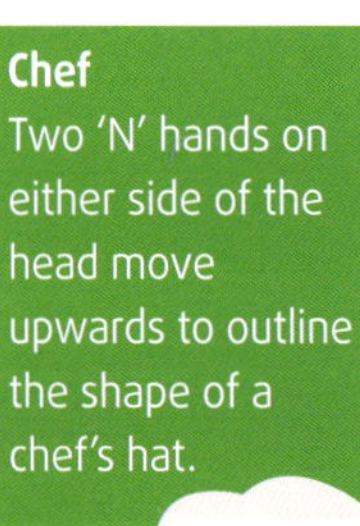

Chop
Flat hands held with palms facing each other and slightly apart. Right hand moves down next to left hand in a chopping motion. Can also be used to indicate 'slice'.

Clear up
Left flat hand with palm facing upwards is brushed clean with blade of flat right hand as if brushing crumbs off a table.

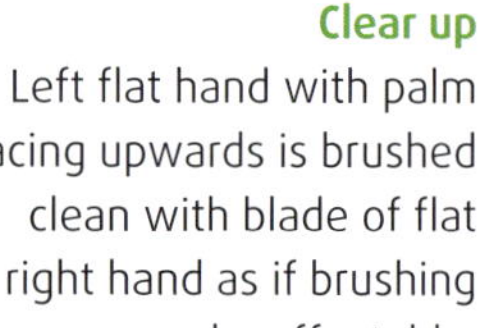

Cook/mix
Left arm mimes holding a bowl whilst right hand mimes whisking ingredients in the bowl.

Cutlery/knife
Two 'N' hands with right hand on top of left at right angles to each other. Right hand moves back and forward in small movements as if sawing. Also the sign for 'knife'.

Danger
Right hand with the palm facing to the left taps twice against the forehead.

Electric
Right hand fist with index finger slightly crooked moves quickly downwards in a zig-zag pattern as if indicating a bolt of lightning.

Fork
Right hand with index and middle finger extended like the prongs of a fork contact the palm of the left hand.

Fridge
Mime grasping a handle and opening the fridge door with your right hand.

Gram
Fingerspell the letter 'G'.

Grill
Flat right hand at eye level with palm facing up moves forward as if putting an item under the grill. Can also be signed at waist level if indicating a grill that is not located at the top of the oven.

Half
Left flat hand facing up. Blade of right flat hand moves back across the left palm towards the body as if dividing something in half.

Gas
Finger spell the letters 'G' 'A' 'S'.

Heat
Clawed hand moves across the mouth from left to right. Also means hot when referring to objects, food and liquids etc.

Jug
Closed hand bends from the wrist and mimes pouring from a jug.

Kettle
Right hand with thumb and little finger extended facing left, tips sideways in a pouring motion.

Kilogram (two part sign)
Finger spell the letters 'K' and 'G'.

Kitchen
Tap the finger spelt letter 'K' together twice.

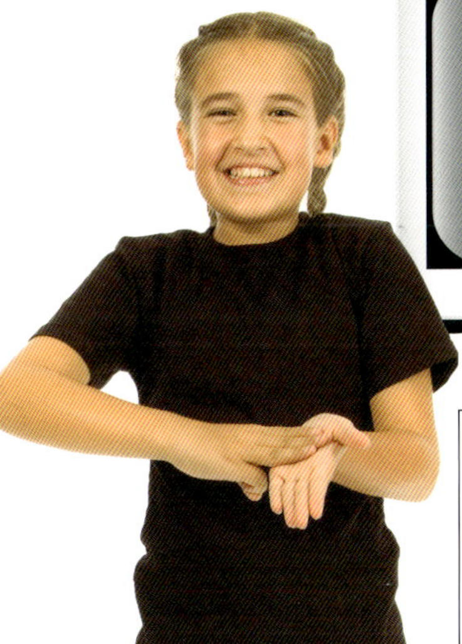

Menu (two part sign)
Finger spell the letter 'M' then move right index finger down the palm of the left hand in small jumps.
Can also be signed in different ways such as miming opening a book.

Microwave (two part sign)
First, finger spell the letter 'M' then bend right hand with fingers facing left. Flex fingers up and down and move from left to right imitating the microwave symbol.

Mug
Mime holding a mug in your right hand with bent thumb extended and mime drinking.

Oven/roast/bake
Two flat hands with palms facing upwards at waist height move forwards as if putting something into an oven. Also can be used for 'bake' and 'roast'.

Plate
Right index finger draws the circular outline of a plate just above the palm of the left hand.

Quarter
Finger spell the letter 'Q'.

Ready
The thumbs of both open hands with palms facing downwards tap twice against the top of the chest.

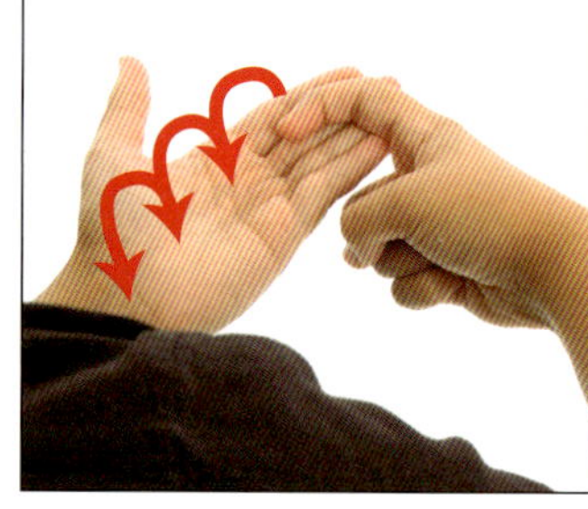

Recipe
Fingerspell the letter 'R' which then moves down the hand in small hops.

Safety
Blade of right flat hand sweeps back towards you across the palm of the left hand.

Saucepan
Mime holding the handle of a saucepan and move hand back and forwards slightly as if moving the pan on the stove.

Scissors
Index and middle fingers of the right hand open and close mimicking the cutting action of a pair of scissors.

Share
The blade of the flat right hand makes short chopping motions back along the length of the upturned flat left hand as if dividing the hand into equal portions.

Shopping
Mime carrying heavy shopping bags in both hands.

Sieve/flour
Right hand mimes holding handle of the sieve and then makes small tapping movements against the palm of the forward pointing flat left hand. Also the sign for 'flour'.

Spoon
Right hand holds an imaginary spoon and moves up towards the mouth.

Steam
Left full 'C' hand with fingers facing right is held still whilst fingers of right hand move upwards through the 'chimney' created by the left hand. Fingers of the right hand slowly open and wiggle like waves of steam.

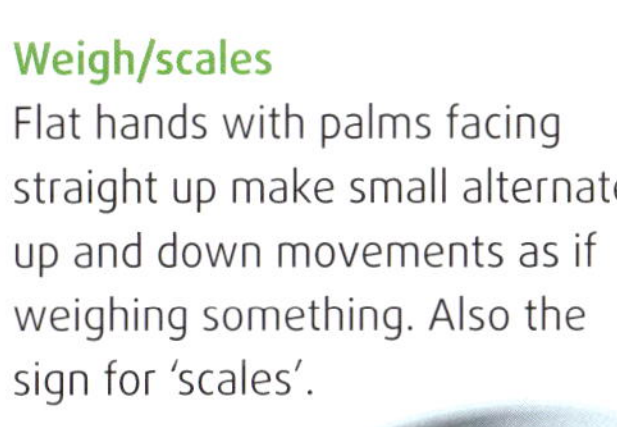

Weigh/scales
Flat hands with palms facing straight up make small alternate up and down movements as if weighing something. Also the sign for 'scales'.

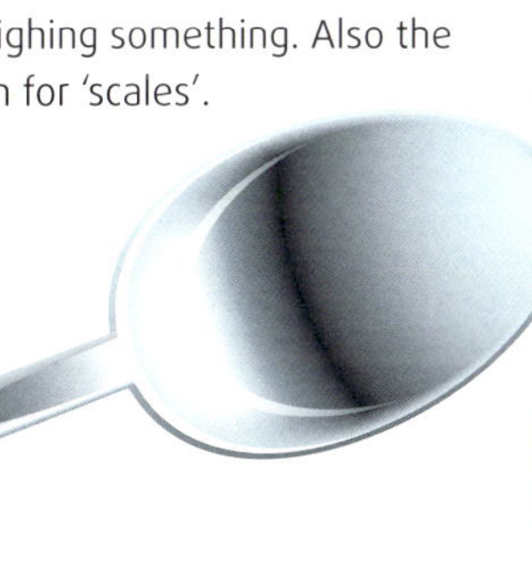

Wash hands
Mime washing hands.

Wash up
Right hand makes small circular movements in a clockwise direction against flat left hand with palm facing right, as if washing up a plate.

Food related signs - vocabulary

Allergy
Right clawed hand scratches up and down left forearm as if scratching a rash.

Bitter
Right fist with index finger extended moves left to right from lips while face shows a sour expression.

Breakfast
Right hand mimes holding a spoon and moves back and forwards towards the mouth.

Coffee
'C' hand held near the mouth, twists backwards and forwards.

Dinner/restaurant
'N' hands move back and forwards to mouth. Also the sign for 'restaurant'.

Drink/juice
Full 'C' hand moves up to mouth as if drinking from a glass.

Food/snack/lunch
The bunched fingers of one hand tap the lips twice, as if eating something. Also the sign for 'snack' and 'lunch'.

Full up/enough/plenty
With bent hand, tap the back of the fingers twice underneath the chin. Also means 'enough' and 'plenty'.

Gravy
Right hand points downwards with index finger and thumb extended and moves in a small clockwise circle in the action of pouring gravy onto a plate.

Hungry
A flat right hand rubs the stomach in a circular motion.

Ice/freezer
Hold both hands in front of you facing downwards. Move them backwards towards your body as if clawing ice.

Ketchup
Left hand mimes holding a sauce bottle, whilst an open right hand slaps twice against the base of the 'bottle'.

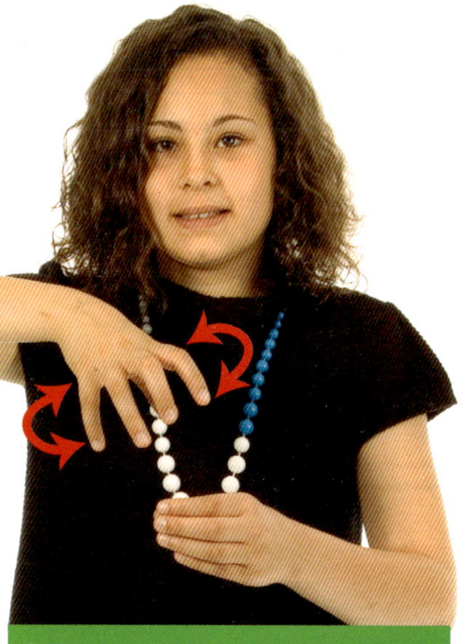

Pepper
Mime grinding pepper from a peppermill.

Picnic
Bunched hands move alternately back and forwards towards the mouth.

Pudding
Right fist with index finger extended describes the shape of a pudding above the left flat hand with palm facing up.

Salad
Both hands with thumbs, index and middle fingers outstretched, mimic the actions of salad tongs tossing a salad.

Salt
Thumb, index and middle fingers rub together as if sprinkling salt onto food.

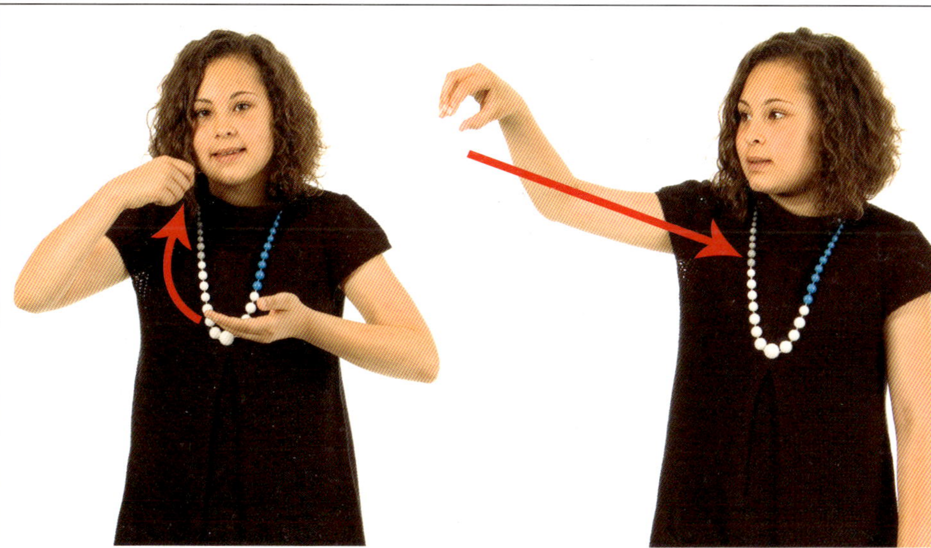

Soup
Left cupped hand mimes holding a bowl, whilst right hand mimes holding a spoon and moves backwards and forwards from the 'bowl' towards the mouth.

Takeaway
Right hand mimes picking up a small bag and moves from right to left.

Tasty
Right fist with thumb pointing upwards moves across the mouth from left to right.

Tea
Left hand mimes holding a saucer whilst the fingers of the right hand delicately hold a tea cup with little finger extended.

Thirsty
Fingers and thumb either side of the throat, move away and down to close into a bunched hand shape.

Water
With an 'O' hand, brush the index finger and thumb down the cheek, twice.

Bread, rice, cereal, pasta, pulses and potatoes - vocabulary

These are called carbohydrates or filler foods. They give us a slow release energy that helps you to keep active for long periods of time. Carbohydrates can be found in all types of bread, crackers, rice and potatoes and also in some vegetables and fruits such as my favourites, bananas. They can even be found in baked beans!

Baked beans
Finger spell the letter 'B' twice.

Bread
Blade of right flat hand slices back and forwards across the face up palm of the left hand as if slicing bread.

Cereal
Left cupped hand mimes holding a bowl whilst right hand mimes holding a spoon and moves backwards and forwards from the 'bowl' to the mouth.

Mashed potato (two part sign)
Right closed hand moves in short up and down 'mashing' movements above flat left hand with palm facing up. Followed by the sign for 'potato'.

Pasta
Two 'V' hands with palms facing up move upwards, 'lifting the pasta from the plate'.

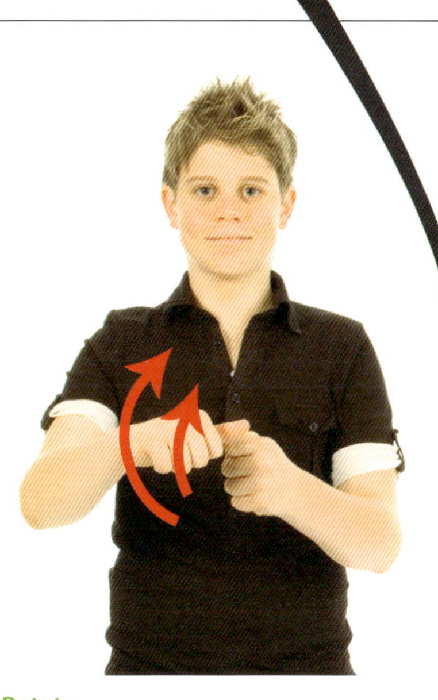

Potato
Left hand is closed into a fist whilst the right hand also closed into a fist with thumb extended to represent a knife, moves backwards and over the left hand in the action of peeling a potato.

Spaghetti
Right fist with thumb extended, pointing downwards, makes small circular movements, 'twisting the spaghetti onto the fork'.

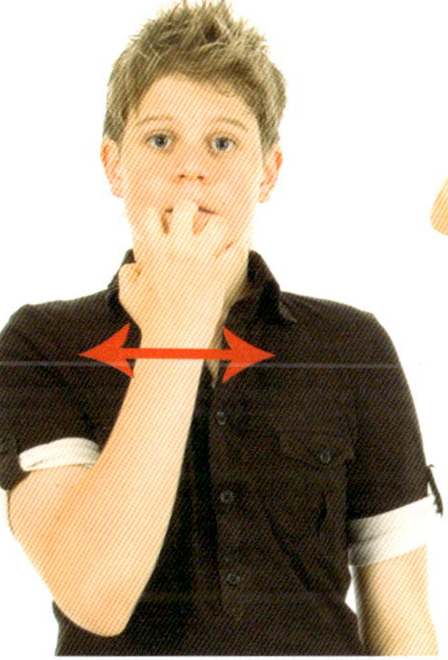

Rice
Clawed right hand shakes side to side in front of the chin.

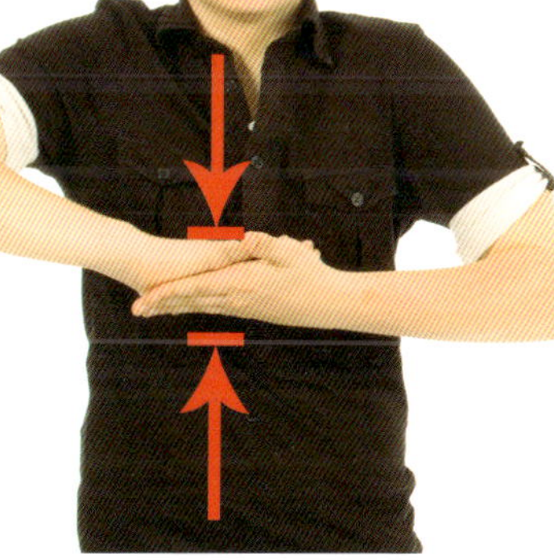

Sandwich
Flat hands held horizontally to the body with palms facing and slightly apart, move together to indicate the two slices of bread in a sandwich.

One potato

One potato, two potato
three potato four
five potato, six potato
seven potato more

Fruit and vegetables - vocabulary

Fruits and vegetables are really good for you because they are full of fibre, minerals and vitamins. To stay healthy it is really important to eat lots of fresh fruit and vegetables. Try eating them as a healthy snack or juicing some into a tasty drink.

Apple
A full 'C' hand mimes holding an apple in front of the mouth and then twists forwards at the wrist as if taking a bite from the 'apple'.

Banana
Mime peeling a banana.

Beetroot (two part sign)
Make a fist using your right hand with index finger extended and slightly bent. Brush the tip of the index finger downwards twice over the lips to make the sign for 'red'. Then use the right index finger to draw the circular outline of the 'root' just above the palm of the left hand.

Blackberry (two part sign)
Sign 'black' by moving a closed hand down the side of the cheek and then add the sign for 'berry'.

Berry

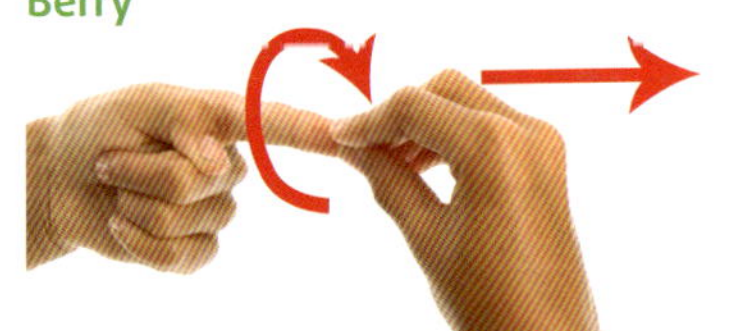

Blackcurrant (two part sign)
Sign 'black' followed by finger spelling the letter 'C'.

Blueberry (two part sign)
Sign 'blue' by using the right index finger to make small back and forth movements on the back of the other hand to indicate blue veins and then add the sign for 'berry'.

Cabbage
Left hand is held into a fist to represent the cabbage. Right flat hand makes downward chopping movements against the 'cabbage'.

Carrot
Right hand mimes holding a carrot near the mouth and then moves sharply downwards as if snapping the 'carrot' with your teeth.

Cauliflower
Right fist, to represent the cauliflower is held against the slightly cupped left hand, which signifies the leaves.

Cherry
Right hand in a 'V' shape pointing downwards at the side of the head, moves slightly from side to side.

Cucumber
Full 'C' left hand mimes holding a cucumber whilst right flat hand makes downward chopping movements as if slicing the 'cucumber'.

Fruit
Full open right hand with wiggling fingers, moves from left to right just below the lips.

Garlic
The fingers of a full open hand wiggle up and down as the hand moves back and forth from the nose.

Grapefruit
Right 'N' hand moves in a small, clockwise circle above a cupped left hand.

Grapes
Both hands in a full 'O' shape touch at the fingertips and then the right hand twists slightly, as if pulling a grape from a bunch and moving it up towards the mouth.

Green Beans
Thumb of the right hand scrapes forwards along the top of a forward pointing left 'N' hand, as if preparing a bean.

Lemon
Right bunched, facing left, hand opens and closes twice at the side of the mouth.

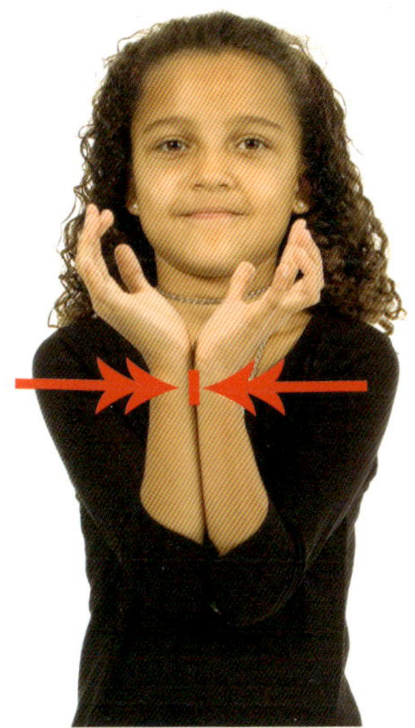

Lettuce
Cupped hands, outlining the shape of a lettuce, tap together twice.

Melon
Full 'C' hands touching together and facing upwards, move apart and curve upwards with fingers and thumbs coming together to describe the shape of a wedge of melon.

Mushrooms
Clawed right hand, facing left, twists slightly back and forwards above the 'stalk' of the 'mushroom', symbolised by the extended index finger of the left hand.

Onion
Index finger brushes lightly twice down the right cheek, just below the eye to indicate tears.

Orange
A clawed hand near the side of the face opens and closes as if squeezing a juicy orange.

Pear
Right 'V' shaped hand is held in front of the mouth with fingers facing left. The hand then twists forwards at the wrist as if taking a bite.

Peas
Right fist with thumb tucked in behind index finger. Thumb then springs up as if flicking a pea across the room.

Pineapple
Open hands touch together at the wrists then move upwards and apart before the wrists touch together again to describe the shape of a pineapple.

Plum
Open left hand, with palm facing forwards. Right full 'O' hand, symbolizing a plum, is held against the tip of the thumb. The right hand twists forwards and away in the action of plucking a plum from a branch.

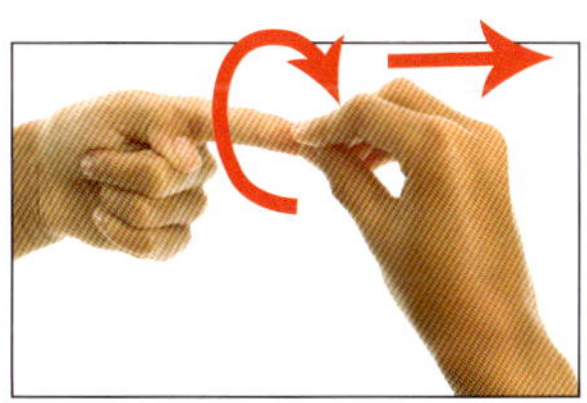

Raspberry (two part sign)

Right fist with index finger extended and slightly bent. Brush the tip of the index finger downwards twice over the lips to make the sign for 'red' and then sign 'berry'.

Rhubarb

Two 'C' hands, held above each other as if holding a stick of rhubarb, move apart in opposite directions.

Strawberry

The tips of the index, middle finger and thumb of both hands contact each other. Then the right hand twists slightly at the wrist and moves away as if twisting the stalk from the strawberry.

Tomato

Two full 'O' hands, with fingertips touching. Right hand twists at the wrist slightly and moves away in the action of removing the stalk.

Vegetable/vegetarian

Right 'V' hand taps the palm of the left hand twice.

Little Jack Horner sat in the corner eating his Christmas pie, he put in his thumb and pulled out a plum And said "What a good boy am I!"

Fats, oils and sugars - vocabulary

Although we need to eat a little fat to help our bodies take in some vitamins, it is important not to eat too many and if possible, look for low fat alternatives. Sugar is instant energy. It gives you a boost, but if you don't burn off the energy by exercising, it can turn into fat. Watch out for the sugar hidden in all those fizzy drinks, biscuits and sweets! Try snacking on a piece of fruit when you feel peckish – it will be better for you and kinder to your teeth too!

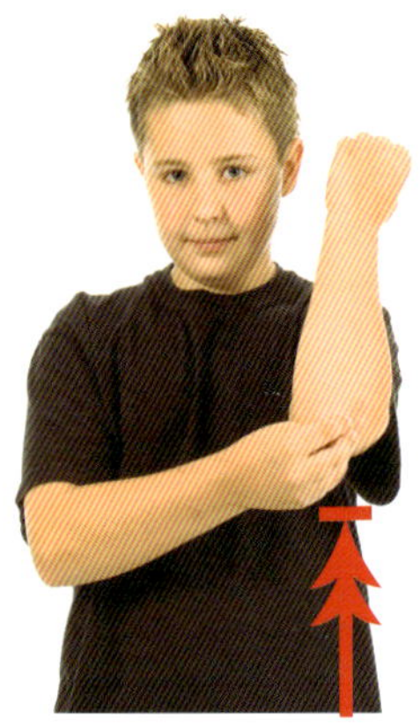

Biscuit
Bunched right hand taps the left elbow twice.

Butter
'N' shaped right hand moves back and forth across the flat palm of the left hand, as if buttering bread.

Cake
Tips of a clawed right hand tap the back of the flat left hand.

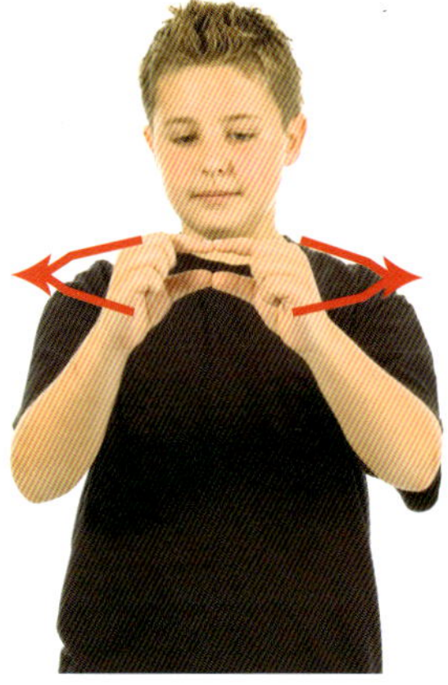

Chips
Index fingers and thumbs of both hands touch each other and move slightly apart as thumb and index fingers close together to show the outline of a chip.

Chocolate
Top part of right 'C' hand touches the chin and moves down to contact the top of the chest.

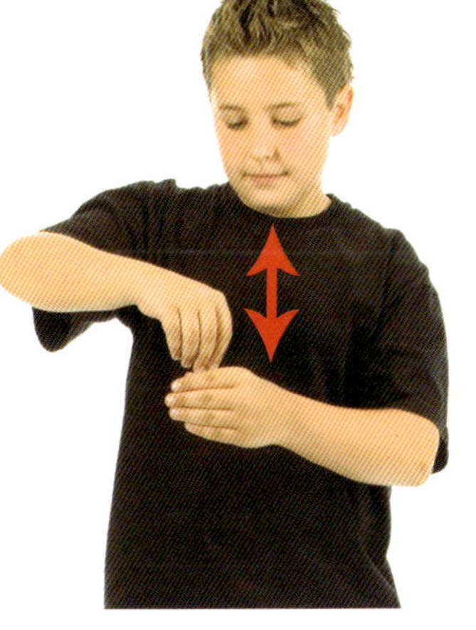

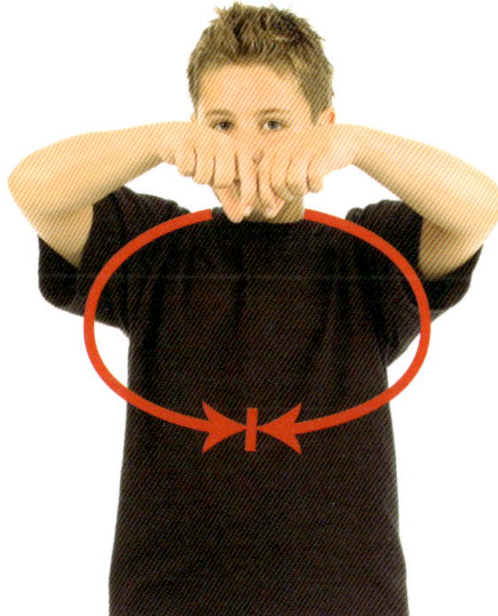

Doughnut
Two full 'C' hands touching, with backs of hands facing upwards, move apart in a small circle describing the shape of a doughnut. Hands end up touching again with palms facing upwards.

Cream
Tip of the little finger of the right hand strokes along the bottom lip as if wiping cream off your lip.

Crisps
Left hand mimes holding a bag of crisps whilst right bunched hand reaches into the bag and moves up to the mouth several times.

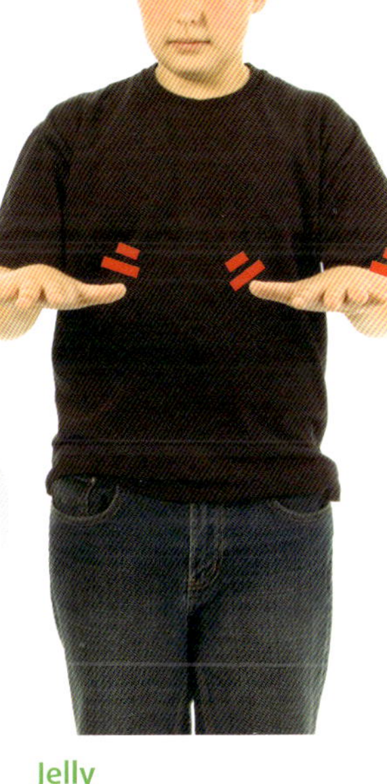

Lemonade
Left hand with fingers and thumb touching makes the shape of a bottle, whilst right open hand with middle finger pointing downwards moves downwards onto the left hand mimicking the action of a stopper going into the neck of a bottle.

Jelly
Open hands with palms facing down shake slightly side to side, imitating the action of a jelly wobbling on a plate.

Ice cream/lolly
A closed right hand makes short downward movements near an open mouth with tongue out, as if licking an ice cream. Also the sign for 'lolly'.

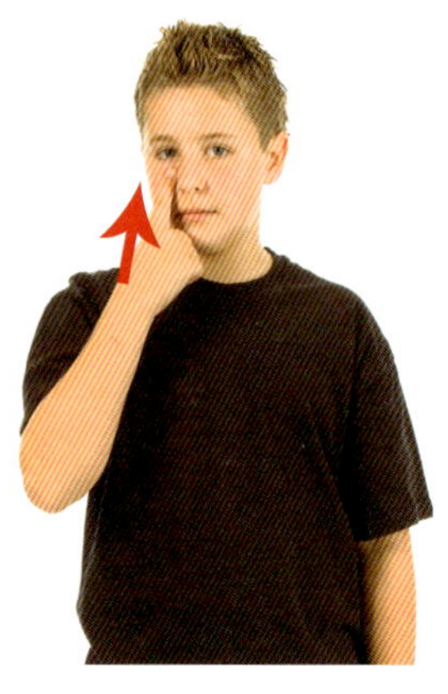

Oil
Right fist with index finger extended moves upwards towards the right eye against the side of the nose.

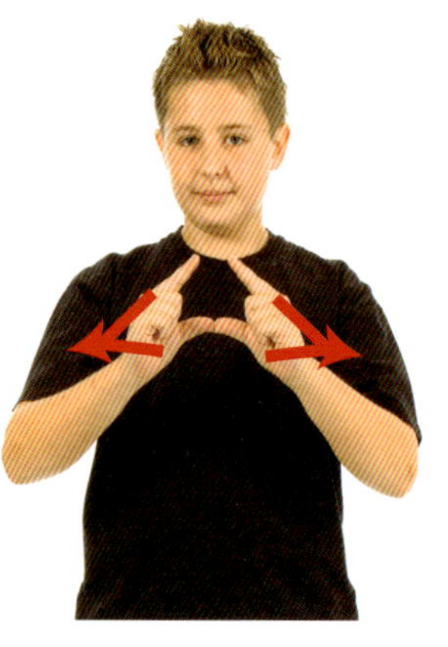

Pastie/samosa
Index fingers and thumbs of both hands touch each other and then move slightly apart as index finger and thumb close together to describe the triangular shape of a samosa.

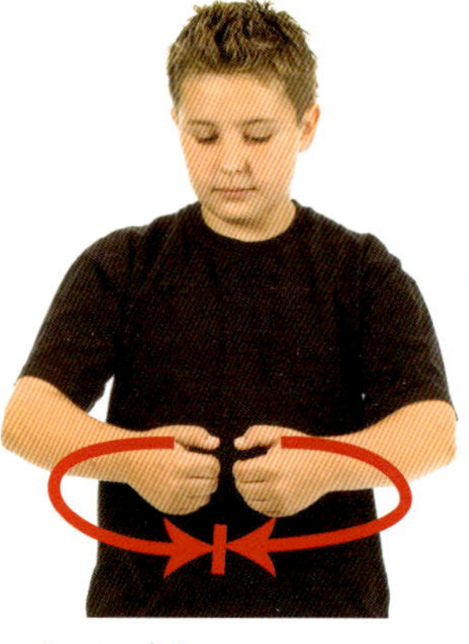

Pastry/pie
Thumbs and index fingers crimp the edges of an imaginary circular pie.

Pizza
Finger spell the letters 'P' and 'Z'.

Sugar
Right 'N' hand with palm facing upwards move slightly from side to side twice.

Sweets
Right index finger touching the cheek with palm facing forwards, twists at the wrist so that the knuckles are facing forwards.

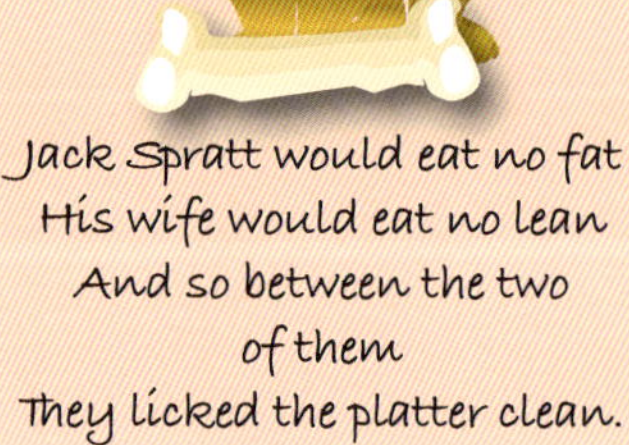

Jack Spratt would eat no fat
His wife would eat no lean
And so between the two
of them
They licked the platter clean.

Jack ate all the lean
His wife ate all the fat
The bone they picked it clean
Then gave it to the cat.

Meat, poultry, fish, nuts and eggs - vocabulary

I love climbing trees, but I need really strong muscles to get to the very top of the tallest trees in the jungle. This group of foods helps to provide us with protein, iron, vitamins and minerals. Protein helps your muscles grow and will help your body repair itself when you get sick or injured.

Bacon
Both 'C' hands pointing downwards, move apart from each other whilst moving slightly up and down to, indicate a floppy rasher of bacon.

Beef
Fist of right hand, with thumb extended jabs, lightly into the side of the neck.

Burger
Two full clawed hands move up to the mouth as if grasping and eating a juicy burger.

Chicken
Index finger and thumb open and close in front of the mouth, in imitation of a beak.

Coconut
Both hands mime holding a coconut up near the head and shaking it, as if trying to hear the milk inside the coconut.

Duck

The fingers of a bunched hand open and close onto the thumb in front of the chin, miming the beak of a duck opening and closing.

Egg

The left hand mimes holding an egg cup whilst the right hand, in an 'N' shape, moves across the top of the left hand as if slicing the top off the egg with a knife.

Fish/fish cake/fish fingers

This sign represents a fish that you eat. The thumb of the right open hand touches the chin as the fingers wiggle. To make the sign for 'fish cake' combine the sign for 'fish' with 'cake'. To sign 'fish fingers' use the sign for 'fish' and then use your index fingers to outline the shape of a fish finger.

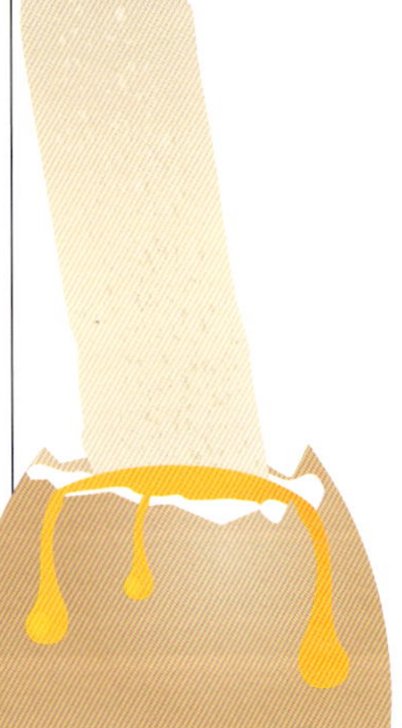

Ham

Finger spell the letters, 'H' 'A' and 'M'.

Hot dog

Both clawed hands mimic holding a giant, curved hot dog in a bun and taking a bite.

Lamb

Fist of right hand, with little finger extended, makes the shape of a ram's horn at the side of the head.

Meat
Right index finger with palm facing forwards, jabs into the neck and twists forward so that the knuckles face forwards.

Nuts/peanut
The heel of the right hand knocks against the underside of the chin twice. To sign 'peanut' you can finger spell the letter 'P' then sign 'nut'.

Pork
A closed fist makes small circles in front of the nose imitating the pigs snout.

Salmon or Tuna
Finger spell the letter 'S' for salmon, or 'T' for tuna, then make the sign for a live fish, using a flat, right hand moving forwards across the body, twisting slightly at the wrist in a swimming motion.

Sausages
Thumbs and index fingers of both hands touch each other, then open and close as they move apart to imitate a string of sausages.

Turkey
Right hand in a 'V' shape moves side to side underneath the chin makes small movements side to side.

Three Fat Sausages

Three fat sausages sizzling in a pan
one went pop and then it went bang.

Two fat sausages sizzling in a pan
one went pop and then it went bang.

One fat sausage sizzling in a pan
one went pop and then it went bang.

No fat sausages sizzling in a pan
None to go pop and none to go bang.

Milk and **dairy foods** - vocabulary

Aren't cows amazing animals? They don't just stand in fields all day eating grass! Cows produce milk which can be turned into all sorts of things, such as smelly cheeses and yummy yoghurt! My favourite though, has to be an extra large banana milkshake! Dairy products are very important for growing children because they provide vitamins, protein and calcium which are good for our bones and teeth.

Cheese
Tips of the fingers of the right flat hand make contact with the upward facing palm of the left flat hand and rock back and forth slightly to represent a wedge of cheese.

Custard
Right hand points downwards with index finger and thumb extended and moves in a small clockwise circle in the action of pouring custard onto a plate.

Milk
Both hands closed, with thumbs held up, move up and down as if milking a cow.

Yoghurt (Two signs)
Finger spell the letter 'Y' then use left hand to mime holding a yoghurt pot whilst the right closed hand with index and middle finger extended, scoops the 'yoghurt 'from the 'pot' and moves towards the mouth.

Hey diddle diddle,
The cat and the fiddle,
The cow jumped over the moon,
The little dog laughed
to see such fun,
And the dish ran away
with the spoon.

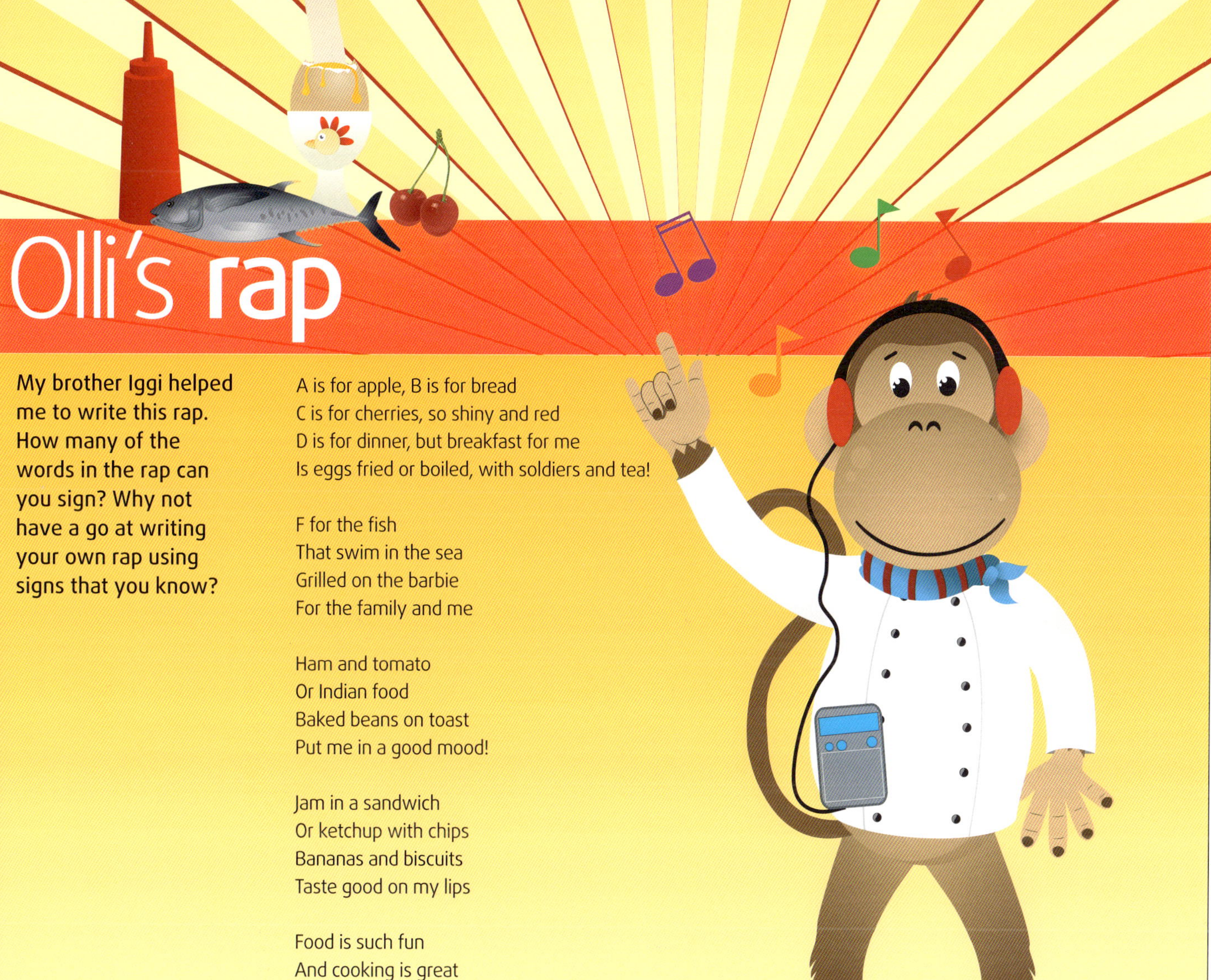

Olli's rap

My brother Iggi helped me to write this rap. How many of the words in the rap can you sign? Why not have a go at writing your own rap using signs that you know?

A is for apple, B is for bread
C is for cherries, so shiny and red
D is for dinner, but breakfast for me
Is eggs fried or boiled, with soldiers and tea!

F for the fish
That swim in the sea
Grilled on the barbie
For the family and me

Ham and tomato
Or Indian food
Baked beans on toast
Put me in a good mood!

Jam in a sandwich
Or ketchup with chips
Bananas and biscuits
Taste good on my lips

Food is such fun
And cooking is great
Join in my rap
And then fill up your plate

I love to eat
And I love to cook
Welcome to all
To the monkey cookbook!

The monkey family **cookbook**

Wash your hands, put on your aprons; it's time to get cooking! Cooking with me couldn't be easier. Just choose a recipe and follow the step by step instructions.

Before you know it, you will be cooking like a professional! Because cooking often involves sharp knives and hot ovens, an adult should be there to supervise at all times.

Olli says:
Ok, have you decided what you want to make? Got all the ingredients? Washed your hands? ...then let's get cooking!

How many bananas?

To help you know which recipes are the easiest to make, I have drawn a banana difficulty rating on each recipe.

If a recipe has a picture of just one banana, it's easy to make. Three bananas mean that it's slightly trickier! Look out for other symbols that indicate whether something is hot or if you need to be really careful.

Weighing and measuring

Weighing and measuring is an important part of learning to cook, and all those numbers will really help with your maths too!

All the recipes use both metric and imperial measurements.

28 grams = 1 ounce

When I cook I use metric, but my Grandad isn't keen on metric and likes to use imperial measurements.

It doesn't matter which one you use as long as you stick with the same system throughout the recipe. Whatever you do don't mix and match grams and ounces!

Teaspoons and tablespoons are used to measure out things like flour or herbs. Make sure that you use the right spoon and that a spoonful of something is flat on the top, not in a great big mound. This is very, very important if you are measuring out something like chilli powder!

To make sure that I don't forget anything, I always measure out all my ingredients at the start.

Monkey macaroons

Simple, quick and tasty, these banana flavoured macaroons are the perfect snack! These are my favourite teatime treat. I often help Mummy to make these. I love the smell of banana flavoured macaroons, warm from the oven!

Banana difficulty rating

(Be careful of the sharp knife and hot oven)

Olli says:
Did you know that bananas don't really grow on trees? Banana plants are actually giant herbs that grow in tropical areas all over the world.

Makes about 30 Macaroons

You will need:

- 2 medium to large sized bananas
- 224g (8oz) self raising flour
- 140g (5oz) butter
- 112g (4oz) castor sugar or sifted icing sugar
- Oil or a little extra butter for greasing
- Pinch of salt

Cooking Equipment:

- Large mixing bowl
- Sieve
- Scales
- Chopping board
- Sharp knife for slicing the bananas
- Table knife
- 2 teaspoons
- Baking tray
- Oven gloves
- Palette knife or spatula
- Wire cooling rack

What to do:

1. Turn on the oven to 180°C/350°F (Gas Mark 4)
2. Sift the flour into the mixing bowl and add the salt.
3. Using your fingers, rub the butter into the flour until the mixture looks like breadcrumbs. This is called 'The Rubbing in Method' and is often used in baking for crumbles, biscuits and scone mixtures.
4. Slice the bananas and add them to the mixture along with the sugar.
5. Mix the ingredients together using the table knife until the mixture begins to stick together.

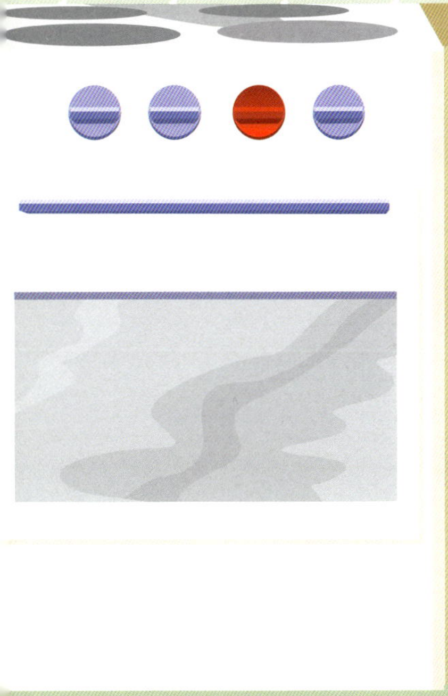

6. Lightly grease the baking tray with oil or a little extra butter.
7. Use the teaspoons to spoon the mixture onto the baking tray into about 30, small biscuit size, portions. Use one teaspoon to divide the mixture and the other to push it off the spoon onto the baking tray.
8. Get an adult to help you put the macaroons into the hot oven using the oven gloves to protect your hands from the heat. The macaroons will need to bake in the centre of the oven for 15 to 18 minutes.
9. Get an adult to help you take the macaroons out of the hot oven. Remember to use the oven gloves to protect your hands from the hot tray. Allow the macaroons to cool on the baking tray for 2 to 3 minutes before using a palette knife or spatula to carefully transfer them onto a wire cooling rack.
10. When the macaroons are cool, store them in an airtight container.
11. The macaroons will keep for about 3 days.

Recipes

Monkey Macaroons

Crocodile crunchies

Banana difficulty rating

(Be careful of the boiling water)

Here's something to really get your teeth into! These crunchy cornflake cakes are made extra special by using white chocolate and green food colouring to give them that scary reptile look!

Makes about 10 crunchy cakes

You will need:

- 140g (5oz) white chocolate
- 84g (3oz) rice and wheat flakes breakfast cereal, bran flakes or cornflakes, or a mixture of all three!
- 2 to 3 drops of natural green food colouring

Cooking Equipment:

- Large heat proof mixing bowl
- Medium sized saucepan
- Wooden spoon
- 2 teaspoons
- Baking tray
- Paper cake cases

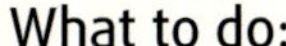

What to do:

1. Arrange 10 paper cases on the baking tray.
2. Get an adult to help you for the rest of this recipe as you will be working with hot saucepans and hot water.
3. Quarter fill the saucepan with cold water and bring it to the boil.
4. Turn down the heat so that the water is simmering.
5. Put a large heat proof bowl onto the top of the saucepan. (The bowl needs to be large enough so that it sits above the water, not in it).
6. Break the white chocolate into small chunks (the smaller the chunks the quicker it will melt!) and put them into the bowl on top of the saucepan.
7. Stir the chocolate in the bowl until it has melted.
8. Put 2 or 3 drops of the green food colouring into the melted chocolate, stirring all the time. (Do not add too much food colouring or the chocolate will become too stiff).
9. Mix the rice and wheat flakes into the mixture, making sure that they are fully coated in the chocolate. Using bran flakes is a great way to get kids to top up on their daily dietary fibre!
10. Use the teaspoons to spoon the mixture into the cake cases.
11. Put the crunchies into the fridge until the chocolate has cooled and is firm.

Iggi's Indian pizza

Make yourself a pizza with a difference! My big brother Iggi makes these really cool pizzas whenever he and his friends fancy a snack. They are different because they use Indian naan bread as a base.

Banana difficulty rating

(Be careful of the sharp knife and hot oven)

Makes four large pizzas

You will need:

- 4 large plain naan breads
- 168g (6 oz) medium Cheddar cheese or buy Mozzarella cheese that has already been grated
- 1 x 454g tin chopped tomatoes
- 3 tablespoons tomato puree
- A large handful of fresh basil and Oregano or 4 teaspoons of dried mixed herbs
- Salt
- Pepper
- Choice of toppings from the list to the right

Cooking equipment:

- Baking tray
- Scales
- Chopping board
- Medium sized mixing bowl
- Small bowl for the grated cheese
- Wooden spoon
- Palette knife or spatula
- Fish slice
- Small vegetable knife
- Cheese grater
- Oven gloves
- Teaspoon

Make your pizza really special by adding 2 or 3 choices of toppings from the list below! You will only need around 56g (2oz) of each topping at the most:

Toppings:

- Sliced mushrooms
- Sliced onions
- Chopped cooked ham, chicken or beef
- Sliced peppers
- Sliced chilli peppers (not too many though or it will be too hot to eat!)
- Sweetcorn
- Tuna flakes
- Pineapple chunks
- Sliced pepperoni or salami
- Prawns
- Baked beans
- Grilled bacon, chopped

Iggi's favourite topping is sliced mushrooms, sliced onion and lots and lots of pepperoni!

What to do:

1. Turn on the oven to 230°C/450°F or gas mark 8.

2. Put the naan breads on a non-stick baking tray.

3. Carefully open the can of chopped tomatoes or get an adult to help you. Then mix together the chopped tomatoes and the tomato puree in the mixing bowl. Finely chop the fresh herbs taking care not to cut your fingers and add to the tomato mixture. Alternatively, add the dried mixed herbs. Stir in the herbs and then divide the mixture between the 4 naan breads. Spread the mixture evenly over the naan breads using a palette knife or spatula.

4. Using the cheese grater, grate the cheese into the small bowl, being careful not to catch your fingers on the grater!

5. Carefully chop and slice the toppings that you want to use.

6. Sprinkle the pizzas with the cheese, then top with the ham, mushrooms or any other toppings that you fancy.

7. Season the pizzas with salt and pepper.

8. Ask an adult to help you, place the pizzas in the hot oven for about 10 minutes until the cheese bubbles (Don't forget to use the oven gloves!).

9. Again, using the oven gloves and with an adult to help you, take the pizza's out of the oven and carefully lift each pizza onto a serving plate using the palette knife or spatula.

10. Serve!

Olli's **lollies**

What better way to cool down on a hot summer day with this fruity drink on a stick! I make these yummy lollies in the same colours as my favourite scarf, using fresh strawberries, raspberries and blueberries.

Banana difficulty rating

(Caution when using electrical equipment!)

Makes about 6 Lollies

You will need:

- 140g (5oz) blueberries
- 140g (5oz) strawberries
- 140g (5oz) raspberries
- 84g (3oz) caster sugar
- 9 tablespoons of water

Cooking equipment:

- Scales
- Blender
- Tablespoon
- 6 lolly moulds

Because fresh fruit is used in this recipe, there are no artificial colours or flavourings used in these lollies. For even healthier lollies, use natural fructose sugar. This can be bought from most supermarkets and natural food shops, or you could even leave out the sugar altogether!

Olli says:

Did you know that ice lollies were invented by an 11-year-old boy called Frank Epperson from California, USA in 1905? Frank had the idea when he accidentally left a soft drink outside on a freezing winter night!

Recipes

Olli's Lollies

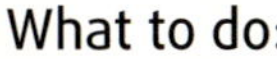

What to do:

1. Put the blueberries, 28g (1oz) of sugar and 3 tablespoons of the cold water into the blender and puree them together.

2. Divide half of the mixture between the six lolly moulds and put the moulds in the freezer to chill. Put the remaining blueberry mixture in a bowl on one side for later.

3. Rinse out the blender.

4. Put the strawberries, 28g (1oz) of sugar and 3 tablespoons of the cold water into the blender and purée them together.

5. Take the lolly moulds out of the freezer and divide the strawberry mixture between them. Put the lolly moulds back in the freezer to chill for about 20 minutes and rinse out the blender.

6. Take the lolly moulds out of the freezer and divide the remaining blueberry mixture between them. Put the lolly moulds back in the freezer to chill.

7. Put the raspberries, 28g (1oz) of sugar and 3 tablespoons of the cold water into the blender and puree them together.

8. Take the lolly moulds out of the freezer and divide the raspberry mixture between them. Insert the lolly mould sticks/bases into the lollies and put back in the freezer until fully set. For best results chill overnight. The lollies will be ready to eat the following day.

9. Once fully set, in order to release the lollies from the moulds, run the outside of the mould under running cold water for a few seconds and then try and ease the lolly out of the case. If it won't move, put it back under the running water for a few more seconds and try again. Keep repeating this until the lolly slides free from the mould.

Grandad's spicy **stuffed peppers**

The chilli powder in this recipe makes these peppers really hot stuff! Grandad loves to show off his exotic cooking skills whenever he comes round for lunch!

Banana difficulty rating

(Be careful of the sharp knife and hot oven)

Olli says:
My Grandad loves chillies! They are really hot and spicy, but actually they belong to the same family as tomatoes and potatoes and contain lots of vitamin A, B, and C.

Serves 4

You will need:

- 1 green pepper
- 1 yellow pepper
- 1 red pepper
- 1 onion
- 56g (2oz) of mushrooms
- 56g (2oz) of cheese
- ½ teaspoon of chilli powder
- Oil for frying
- Salt
- Pepper

Cooking equipment:

- Scales
- Chopping board
- Cheese grater
- Sharp knife for preparing vegetables
- Baking tray
- Wooden spoon
- Medium sized pan
- Oven gloves
- 2 Bowls
- Tablespoon

Suitable for vegetarians

Recipes

Grandad's spicy stuffed peppers

What to do:

1. Cut all of the peppers in half on the chopping board using the knife. Take out all of the seeds and as much of the white pith as possible and wash the pepper halves.
2. Put the yellow and red pepper halves onto the baking tray. These will be used as a sort of serving dish and filled with the spicy mixture.
3. Finely chop the green pepper halves and put in a bowl to one side.
4. Chop the onion as finely as you can, taking care not to cut your fingers! Add the onions to the diced green pepper.
5. Slice the mushrooms and add them to the bowl containing the green peppers and onion.
6. Weigh out the cheese and carefully grate it into a separate bowl. Watch out for your fingers when grating cheese!
7. Put a tablespoon of oil into a medium sized pan and place on the cooker hob over a medium to high heat. You might want to ask an adult to help you do this.
8. Once the oil is hot, add the chopped vegetables and chilli powder and keep stirring until the pepper is soft and the onion is just turning a golden brown colour.
9. Add the grated cheese and mix until the cheese has melted.
10. Divide the mixture between the red and yellow pepper halves. Get an adult to help you put the pepper halves into an oven that has been pre-heated to 200°C/400°F or Gas Mark 6.
11. Bake for 20 minutes. When the 20 minutes are up, carefully remove the peppers from the oven, using oven gloves to protect your hands from the hot tray.
12. Use a fish slice to lift the peppers onto plates.
13. Serve with a side salad, allowing one pepper half per person. If you're feeling really hungry serve two pepper halves per person.

Index of signs

KITCHEN CLOSED
CHEF'S DAY OFF!

yum
NEW
CEREAL
CEREAL
CEREAL
CEREAL
CEREAL

About the **author**

Garry Slack is a fully qualified Communication Support Worker for deaf people and has extensive experience of supporting both deaf and deaf-blind people in many different situations.

He has developed and delivered sign language and non verbal communication workshops to people of all ages, including parents, children, young people and professionals.

As well as devising the 'Learn to sign with Olli' series, Garry is a freelance trainer and speaker on non verbal communication, working in partnership with several local authorities throughout the UK.

When he isn't teaching or writing, Garry lives a quiet life in Lincolnshire with his partner and four noisy sausage dogs!

Olli says:
I hope you've enjoyed cooking with me and hope we can learn something new next time

A big **thank you**

I would like to thank all the people who have helped with this project.

Thank you to Ross Burden for writing the foreword.

Thanks to Matt Maddock for taking the fantastic photographs. Paul Collings, the Youth Theatre Officer at Peterborough City Council. The models, Tom, Michael, Taryn, Katie, Rene, Colleen, Joe and their families. New College Stamford for the use of their photographic studio. Sue Otter, Early Years and Childcare Training Officer at Lincolnshire County Council. Richard S, Karis, Steve, Mel and Richard T at dsquared for their outstanding design and Sharon Seel with her eagle eyes. Hazel Cushion and the team at Accent Press for their belief and support. Neville and Glenys Walkley, Trustees of Deaf Lincs for their friendship and continued support, and a special thank you to John Orrill, MIH (Member of the Institute of Hospitality), for developing and testing the recipes.